A FAILED ATTEMPT AT UNDOING MEMORIES
DARE TUNMISE

This is a work of fiction. All names, characters, places, and incidents are a product of the author's imagination. Any resemblance to real events or persons, living or dead, is entirely coincidental.

Published by Akashic Books
©2024 Dare Tunmise
ISBN: 978-1-63614-216-6

All rights reserved
Printed in China
First printing

Akashic Books
Instagram, X, Facebook: AkashicBooks
info@akashicbooks.com
www.akashicbooks.com

African Poetry Book Fund
Prairie Schooner
University of Nebraska
110 Andrews Hall
Lincoln, Nebraska 68588

TABLE OF CONTENTS

Preface by Tjawangwa Dema 5

Inheritance 9
Ode to my mother 11
A failed attempt at undoing memories 12
Resurrection 14
Dear Departed 16
Of strangers and bleeding bones 18
Trench 19
Centos as midnight prayers 21
Beloved 22
Flowers and Dark Rooms 23
Starless Night 24
Elegy for a body who drowned 25

Acknowledgments 27

PREFACE
by Tjawangwa Dema

Nigerian poet Dare Tunmise's chapbook contends with memory in two ways simultaneously, as both an archiving site and a project of failure. Here we are "eyes closed, but [. . .] not sleeping." What does it mean to write from memory? I suspect the binary we build between memory and what is before us, in other words, prospective memory that is registering and building itself, begets failure. Surely, one pulls from the other as Tunmise's "ghost skips a room." ("A failed attempt at undoing memories") You say the car before you is red because you remember what the color red and a car look like. But what, Tumise's poems seem to ask, must one be longing for or haunted by to make a home of memory, which is itself only a holding place?

> I rubbed myself in coriander, and asked, "Father,
> am I not tender for this offering?"
> [. . .] what do we bear in our names if not someone's failed
> attempt to fill emptiness?
> ("Inheritance")

Tunmise writes in praise of memory's complexity and resilience. He is mindful of the ways in which memory stores and is the store; the ways in which it is beholden to naming and ordering, as well as how it re-presents reality. As a software developer, he is likely aware of how we grapple to retrieve things from the margins. However, the poet in him knows that literary memory is a fickle project, as bound to fact as it is to fabulation. His speakers' sense of memory, as something that doesn't loop but oscillates, is telling. Memory does not necessarily align itself with what is coherent or complete. It comes and goes, and its ability to be retrieved shifts with time. What memory finds present or absent, it colors or completes, echoing any silence back to us as an inability to remember.

> And it is only in these photographs that we have remained a herd, before the desert came calling our names with the promises of exiles. Before you signed your names to a war calling you because war is the only song found worthy in the tongue of home. ("Dear Departed")

Memory makes songs of the obviously spectacular—war, death, labor, and so on. It heightens and colors, reordering time so that we might be shown the dead and immediately think of "wine and mischief," of birds, anything but the dying body itself. ("Dear Departed") The poet understands connections, therefore he chases and corrals not only sweeping memory but mundane memories too. For it's possible that the true function of memory lies not in its perfect or grand recollection, but rather its signification—what was felt? And why the impetus to remember this and not that?

We are of course attached to our perspectives, practiced in our gaze from our upright human positions, but we too fall within memory:

> On the eve of your leaving,
> we sat on the blocks outside your home, shared a bottle of wine
> before mapping our feet through boroughs and alleys
> of a street that knew us like childhood memories.
> ("Trench")

We delimit and imagine ourselves at the center. But we too are objects that are seen by what we look at, by the birds who bear "witness to the sadness / in our eyes." We too live in memory, it is one of our homes.

With reference to "half-finished poems" and the silence within them, it's clear that the speaker is aware that he's a poet. He is engaged in an exercise of imagination *and* alive in the world. Tunmise risks pointing to the act of narration (whether by human or fish) even as his speakers summon from their own memories the landscapes of shepherds and Christ, unnamed migrants made nameless at sea, and the sea itself (or whatever waters bloat houses and harbor "the remains of dead ships"). Perhaps he risks what he knows is underwritten by working with not just metaphorized stories, but an existing archive that gestures to Lagos, Tobruk, Ibadan, and his own young and incomplete archive of memory: "but the ocean I built with you who left is empty of ships and I do / not seek for a canoe to take me home." ("Dear Departed")

What we remember matters mostly to us unless we are witness to a crime or historical happening. If we mean to gather and leave words behind for others to find, then perhaps it matters how the Nigerian, not Motswana or American, sees Lagos's "blues." "Shattered" or not, here the blues are affixed on the page for whoever should wish to re/collect them in the future. So perhaps it is a good thing that the poet remembers he is a poet, that he is attentive to the ways in which memory resists flame or willful renunciation. It is a good thing that poetry is a part of that resistance.

Poetry, it may be argued, is subjected to the laws of scalability. The worlds of poems must be economical—there is only so much of an eon, a city, a girl that can fit into a poem. Yet the reader will bring their experience and biased expectation in search of something contained within but also bigger than the poem. A complex cage for a poem perhaps, "but," Tunmise writes, "what sings in the cage tonight is not a dove thirsty for water, / nor that a bird of ritual seeks to break free." The poet can only ask, "where is the place of sacrifice?" ("Inheritance") If the poem is a boat ferrying us somewhere, the poems' speakers suggest that we sacrifice part of the recalled journey in order to give our reader the familiar shape of a poem, by "crossing the ocean on a boat built / with eggshells and feathers of quails." ("Resurrection")

Memory travels beyond us collecting what it may until, to undo it, we have to undo ourselves. After all, in their sincere and contemplative tone, Tunmise's speakers tell us that "to erase memories, you must kill a name." ("A failed attempt at undoing memories") Pushing his name out to sea amid the growing canon of African voices, Tunmise's *A Failed Attempt at Undoing Memories,* as poetry and as a grappling with personal and public memory, is consecration and naming.

INHERITANCE

When a mother bestows a name on her child, it reveals her hope.
—Langston Hughes

Before the consecration,
I was a light lost in my mother's womb,
and my father touched my eyelids and said,
Son, you were not named after the sea to sight
rain and cave your body under a hill.

And it is only through these words that I have come to regard myself
as a god in my mother's understanding of clay.

The baptist said all that touched water had been made holy,
but I know, I know the guilt of pebbles is that they must carry the sea
within their veins, and in the shore is the dark history of rivers,
and how they were once mirrors before telling their secrets to sands for liquid pity.

I have walked barefoot on this road that I may shed this history behind me,
kept a bonfire in my mouth to keep the wolves away from the door.

But what sings in the cage tonight is not a dove thirsty for water,
nor that a bird of ritual seeks to break free.

And where is the place of sacrifice?

And after smoothing the knife, I rubbed myself in coriander, and asked, "Father, am
I not tender for this offering?"
It is how a sacrificial lamb knows its place in the midst of a herd,
or what do we bear in our names if not someone's failed attempt to fill emptiness?

I have seen a city named after a rock to preserve the memory of its forebears.
I have seen a girl named after her mother who died during childbirth.
I was born and my own father named me Tunmise—a sort of safety boat meaning;
the child was born after a shipwreck.
The ghosts of a generation line under my bones and
I still haven't found a grave to lay them.
Once, in the dark, I asked the lines in my palms where they lead.
And one opened into a city of dry flowers asking me
to speak like God in the voice of rain.

ODE TO MY MOTHER

In this poem everything else is silent,
but not the wall clock chiming rhythm
like memory waiting to complete an oscillation.
The mark on the almanac on the wall says it's
three years since the fire, and here you are, Mother,
asleep with the calmness of a rod ready to create a path in the sea.
But I do not begrudge the bent stick that is now
your left pinky finger, it is how many times you have
held embers in your hand, how many time you have lifted
your child out of the fire and said, salt, water, live.
Outside this page, I have been dead once, saw what lay between heaven and hell;
not a purgatory, but the science of how a body can isolate itself and stick
to one silent note—the language of the dead, the language of a lamb
first learning a knife. And what does the shepherd do but watch
the treachery of the blade on what it loves?
The man on the cross screaming, *eloi eloi eloi,* but unlike
you, my Mother, who knew the music to call the phoenix out of fire,
who knew what to sing with the ashes still burning on your tongue.
And what has healed in this poem is not the body learning to crawl
out of grief, but the secret that is the redemption found
with a sheep washing blood off a lamb with its tongue.
After the fire, you said this flower shall bloom.
And at the end of this poem, a rainbow shoots out of a dark place.
You renamed it Damascus; the journey of how a boy's body gathered itself
in his mother's palm to find himself.

A FAILED ATTEMPT AT UNDOING MEMORIES

Eyes closed, but you're not sleeping.

It is your shadow screaming to the walls
as the candle burns into a slow fade.
Said something is dead inside you,
but you would not touch a wound,
wash a ghost clean till it's all paradise
in a room made unholy with sex and wine.

The stained white tissue on the bed
that mocks holiness, calls voyage to a night sky
without a moon, and a half sea swallowed
in your bones that wash in memories
like the brevity of thunder caught
on a baby's tongue as he coughs out blood
on his mother's lap. It says there is enough music
in this silence if you would listen to the walls
as a ghost skips a room, if you would observe
the wall gecko driving time back as the woman
with wound screams in labor in an empty kitchen.

Eyes closed, but you listened as a boy swallowed
wine and ate history like burnt cars on his father's lips,
and because nothing would bring water to the wreckage
of the toy he burned on a candle as the wax bled
like snow into an empty tin. Except that the remains
of those nights sat in his books as stories bruised
at the edges because no one could bring back
the child he found dead asleep in a neighbor's house.

Because no one could tend the dog's wound
till the sore became the symphony the rots sang
to sleep on its hind legs. Eyes closed, but he would maintain
an autonomy of these griefs and paint them as lost words
looking for rooms on random pages because he would not
pretend that the world is a slow herb that requires little burning,
that he would one day sleep in an empty room
and scream out of sleep as he remembered the image
of the boy he played with burning in a room
while his father's fist rammed into the woods for open door.

Eyes closed, but the morning would not begin
with a new song because he would not know
that to erase memories, you must kill a name.

RESURRECTION

I don't know who filled the roof of this house with
fertile eggs,

but the crows now are hatching in moist nests,
and I've had my body filled with the blood of dead moths.

My mother is sitting here; she's not the one.
There are tears in my sisters' eyes;
they are not crying.

My father said "live" before his shadow disappeared
into the white beam of a doorpost.

Meanwhile, the guardian angel has left
the house foot, swollen with grief.

Meanwhile, I'm crossing the ocean on a boat built
with eggshells and the feathers of quails.

The thing about passing out is how you keep
thinking you have never left,

drifting into the sea with the songs of relatives standing at the
bank, waiting for your dead to navigate their own arrival.

In the hospital,
I woke up sneezing and my lids became heavy with half-formed
memories.

If the doctor was to sigh, it would be displayed as the EKG
graphing toward rough angles.
On a normal day, I would have smiled
and told him death is only a silence prolonged by rivers,

but I am not sure if the nurse fixing the drip asked if they've
renamed the last sea after God.

There's a new sun rising in my mother's face as a child coughs
himself out of sleep,

and there's no word to paint the prayer on her lips or the depth
of her whispers to my ear that her palm has been holding fire for my body to
mend of its broken stitches.

DEAR DEPARTED

We have nowhere to go, but we are leaving anyhow,
by many ways.
—Tyree Daye, "From Which I Flew"

And answer this:
if departure would be the end of us,
where do we go writing maps in the footprints of
friends who left home before midday?
I'm looking through the photographs of old friends
and picking silence where absence sits like rocks in the vacancy of names.

And it is only in these photographs that we have remained a herd,
before the desert came calling our names with the promises of exiles.
Before you signed your names to a war calling you because
war is the only song found worthy in the tongue of home.
There are no days I wake up without thinking about the sea
and its endless lists of drowned voyages.
And my mouth singing memories would not stop a boat and
our old promises to keep the flotsam awake with psalms.

Tonight, the news from Tobruk speaks of migrants found dead
floating the face of the sea but nobody gives a name.
Another headline speaks of ambushed soldiers
found dead in a war our country's silence would not
stop from asking for blood and more blood.

Tonight, in the possibilities of roads, I journeyed towards Time,
but stars of exiles do not seek reunions in a moonless sky.

I do not know if fishes get to narrate their own exiles, I do not ask,

but the ocean I built with you who left is empty of ships and I do
not seek for a canoe to take me home.

Dearly departed,
I do not want the waves to bring you home to a funeral led
by birds,
I long for a night of wine and mischief while we drink of the grief
and joy embedded in those moments unshared in our undiscovered exiles.

OF STRANGERS AND BLEEDING BONES

Outside dreams, there are no rooms
for wandering bones, except the spaces
in water to harbor the remains of dead ships.
And we heard they don't bury the bodies of strangers.
The city said it leaves them cold in the country's outskirts
till they become old like fossils in open museums,
cheap warnings for those who will not find peace in leaving.
I have poured a river of incense in the room.

Tonight, we will feast with a legion of faces that knew
us like a childhood song, rub kohl tenderly to soften faces,
the meats in the mouth of Alsatians that stop them from barking
away the ghost of strangers.
Remember to meet me in that place of dream, I'll be soft like memories
to welcome you here, where griefs are crumpled flowers
gathered in the mouth of sharks as we walk back again into that bar,
where we drank from the rims of rusted cups before you slipped
your passport into my palm and whispered that our country
is a quarantine of dead and collected dreams.
We will speak again of departure.
And do not ask me of your mother. I will not know how to describe
a house falling into water.
I will not know how to speak the grief of a woman
watching knives sharp as graves digging into her son
as the soil below him becomes a factory of red, thick and liquid things.
Do not ask me of home because I will not know how to tell of sisters
sinking into the edges of sofas, of old friends turning eyes away
while we gather around the TV to watch a migrant butchered
to death in an unnamed street faraway in South Africa.

TRENCH
For L.O. Olajide, who fought at the operation Lafiya Dole

I
On the eve of your leaving,
we sat on the blocks outside your home, shared a bottle of wine
before mapping our feet through boroughs and alleys
of a street that knew us like childhood memories.
And the birds of that evening bore witness to the sadness
in our eyes, and your mouth heavy with departure;
the forlornness of home deep in your voice, which leaving
would not separate from the future of days wet with blood
and sores and memories of home and the scars of bullet wounds.

II
Later that night, in my house, we sat over dinner
and you passed the meats to us saying, eat, drink, not only in
remembrance of you, but like Christ dipping his ribs into salt
for every scribe sitting at the table waiting on his flesh.

III
But these days,
we heard there are soldiers dying in Borno,
of mass and undisclosed graves of men buried in the heat of battle,
of flowers dying in the cold of graves, the unmarked tombs
of men fighting to certain death.

IV
And these days, the wind breaks each voice trying to call Borno.
We heard that the blood is wet over telephone wires,
that there are messages stranded in the air where soldiers sit in
death speaking their last.

V
And each day I stand at the newsstand,
reading tolls of death, grotesque bodies in newspapers.
I'm skipping all names that start with O or L
because my grief doesn't know a name.
And I'm too scared to see the death of a friend killed in the cold of war,
an AK-47 clutched to his chest with his body lifeless on bloody ground
in a city far away from the warmth of home.

CENTOS AS MIDNIGHT PRAYERS

Lord,
forgive me for the birds dying inside my eyes,
for my horses growing wild,
for the flowers burning on my tongue as the rain hit the ground,
for the flies learning darkness as the light goes out,
for the midnight dog as it calls ghosts away from the procession of crows,
for this darkness as it looms over the churchyard,
for the child watching from behind the door as a priest undoes a nun,
for the girl at the convent learning to touch herself in new ways.

Forgive us for this beast as a man gropes his daughter in a dark room,
for the moan floating over the water as it crosses into the night dark.

Forgive this errant body waiting at the alley,
for the cop as he undoes his holster,
for the flesh, water, and marrow as they meet in the core secret of a bone,
for the mob as it rises to mark a skin,
for the bodies going up in flames that wouldn't break you into rain,
for the refugee boat and the travelers that would be spared the safety of the coast,
for the things left behind and the purity of the morning as the earth crosses into
    a new day,
for the song and grief as it leads a boy toward a rope,
for this prayer
and the silence of each dying thing like me that wouldn't reach you.

BELOVED

There are many lovers holding hands tonight,
but I am outside the house singing
as the radio plays Nina Simone, and not songs of aloneness,
but songs of the longing to fill the vacancy that makes
light soft enough to walk into a bone,
and of the thirst that makes a butterfly cross a sea
to be swallowed in the nectarine attitude of wildflowers.
In the silence that follows the emergence of stars
as a new moon takes over the skyline,
I am here listening to the joint chorus of two birds.
But they do not sing of us, and nothing in the science
of their flight can tell of our wildness,
nothing that can imitate the crooked music leaving
our mouths in the blasphemy of bodies every night we search
for God in the nooks of our own skins.
I do not ask if silence is what answers when absence calls a name.
Tonight, I'm doodling on the scrap of half-finished poems as I seek
for a tightness akin to the taut skin of a plum.
But do you think of me in the completeness you do not find
in the deep tongues of men seeking ways into your name in the nooks
of Lagos and its shattered blues,
in the hollowness that plants itself in the tongues
of birds when they can't reach the water?
Ibadan is cold and the holes are getting wider,
but the birds would not stop singing of desires.
In the room, I break myself into a god drunk in desires,
with the fantasy of moaning your name out of wet dreams.

FLOWERS AND DARK ROOMS
If I told you that a flower bloomed in a dark room, would you trust it?
—Kendrick Lamar

He said, "How do flowers grow from walls that
don't speak the language of water?"
And you said, "By shedding tendrils bruised with saps or
forging their way through layers of granite and rustic stones."
I see you searching for lights cutting holes
out of large rocks.
The photosynthesis of those pigments that become sparks
shine you through layers of grime and conflicting dreams.
Where we live, mother told us to keep our tongues invisible like dreams.
She said moths will become butterflies
if only they hide their wings in the dark of a house far from fire.
I held mine in the pages of old books,
a catalogue of scriptures kept in a box where father saved them
for history to sip through each letter.
It was how I learned to grow with memories that left scars in my head.
In houses closer to mine,
I know boys drowning now in the debris of dead liquor,
or girls hiding babies in bellies bigger than the stool of God.
I once rode on my father's tongue before he said,
"The way out of our street led through a path the size of a needle's eye."
I have been searching for a map out of this geography of flytraps,
and there are other flowers falling in dark rooms
without reaching the taste of the sun.

STARLESS NIGHT
For Fikayo

And not even the contemptuous cries of crows
could lighten a night that has come out starless,
and in the place of a half-moon, a lone satellite is crashing out of space
as I peeped outside the window, where, again,
the lone bird began a song as I followed its dirge to the dark of
a café filled with the bones of a dead child.
I knew this was how your mother must have felt as she threw
the last of your clothes in fire
for a memory that would not die in flame.

In the quietness of a voiceless night,
I remember tossing you in the air outside
your grandmother's house in Alakia.
Your set of first teeth glistens in chuckles
brighter than the washed pebbles of the sea,
but I do not beg to remember you this way.
The grief that steals a child from the grip of its mother,
and the innocence of an infant skin craft in burial,
in the pale inglorious garment of quicksands.

When flowers die, they give their ashes to the clay,
I want a wind to sweep through this valley
and speak as God walking through dry bones,
or the innocent cry of a child more beautiful than the grave
growing mold in your mother's throat as she places flowers
on your gravestone.

ELEGY FOR A BOY WHO DROWNED
For Odunare Olalekan

Before you found the water,
you sat at the edge of a bloated house,
waiting for a safety that does not look like the inferno burning the ship
in the dream where you're trying to hold your skin from falling off a cliff,
and it was here like a ritual, you
committed yourself to silence and jumped into the lagoon,
but your end does not begin where you look at the place
where the world burn, and there was no hand to hold you because
the anchor was melting into a magma,
another cast for the boat that would sink into the mouths
of those who will say depression does not kill a man,
that it is not enough to tow a chick into the cold
mouth of a wolf, and those who after your death
would mutter that life goes on.

I have carried this grief within me the way a dog carries
hunger in its belly, and rehearsed as echoes barked through
empty halls.

But even now with your body giving itself to salt;
hallowed be the core interior part of your body,
the unseen inside, where last night, you turned the soil
and buried a dead horse,
and your wet bird screaming could not find an anchor to lift it to the air,
because the sea level kept rising.

Hallowed be the boats you built from rib bones
as they sink because your teeth could no longer hold them.

Hallowed be the thought of your humans
as they're torn below the surface of the sea,
and Hallowed be this water, your imagined safety as it washes
you into the core deep of the ocean where breathing
is easy for a body lifting itself out of fire.

ACKNOWLEDGMENTS

The following poems have appeared in these publications: "A failed attempt at undoing memories" in *IceFloe Press*; "Resurrection" in *Sublunary Review*; "Flowers and dark rooms" and "Strangers and Bleeding bones" in *The Kalahari Review*.